Premonitions of the Palladion Project

A Modern Project Management Fable

Scott S. Haraburda, PhD, PE

To my eternal soulmate. Your love burns brightly in my heart and lives forever. May all of our dreams or premonitions come true.

———————

Contents

Preface

I worked on several different kinds of projects throughout my career, both as a project member and as the project leader (or manager). Some of my projects involved commanding thousands of Soldiers, developing & running a large scale military training exercise, destroying weapons of mass destruction for the US Government, installing an innovative "real-time" industrial measurement system for a Fortune 5 US-owned company, installing new production equipment for a large international foreign company, or planning a family vacation. Several of these projects were successful while others were not. With this experience, I observed successful project managers use wrong project tools, and have seen unsuccessful managers use "state-of-the-art" project tools.

Being inquisitive, I asked the question of "why did this happen?" More specifically, how could project managers execute successful projects using the wrong project tools; and likewise, how could project managers execute unsuccessful projects using the best project tools? My questions contradicted the project management experts advertising that their tool would revolutionize the project business by making one successful in running a project. Do not get me wrong. I believed that project tools were important. My general thesis was that using just the best project management tools while forgetting everything else about running the project would doom the project to failure.

To avoid managing unsuccessful projects, I continually gathered information about what worked and what did not work when managing a project. This was my personal "lessons learned" program for continual self-improvement. I firmly believe that using this information could assist anyone in managing a more successful project.

With this self-improvement information, I fabricated a fable to provide a project management framework illustrating twenty-four of these lessons. Using the concept of **The Defence of Duffer's Drift** (D3) tale, my fable is titled **Premonitions of the Palladion Project** (P3). Major General Sir Ernest Swinton wrote D3 a century ago, which eventually assisted the US Army in teaching infantry tactics to its leaders. The intent with my fictional tale was to accomplish something similar for the art of project management with my P3 story.

———————

Prologue

It was Thursday morning, and I had just finished my project management course, ready and eager to use my newly acquired project management tools. I needed this course to learn about the tools and skills necessary for success in my next job. Prior to beginning this course a few months ago, I was selected for a key project management position. However, it wasn't until last week that I was told which project I was going to manage, a project I had never heard about.

After that important phone call notifying me of my selection as the project manager for the Palladion Project, I did not know what to think, especially about this project. All that I could think about at the time was that this project involved an exotic chemical. I remembered hearing about a similar name, palladium, from my general chemistry class in college. Not being a scientist or even an engineer, I could not imagine someone selecting me for a chemically related project.

After several days researching this project in the school's acquisition-based library, I discovered that this project was a multi-million dollar defense survivability system that was used primarily by the defense industry. It even involved several significant civilian commercial applications too. The project was currently in the research & development phase with the current goal of developing a prototype of this survivability system. I further learned that this project involved some state-of-the-art technologies, such as satellite communications, remote sensors, complex computer systems, and associated survivability hardware. There was also something about net-centric warfare – whatever that was. I began to wonder why I was selected. It was probably a dart-board selection process.

I further discovered the logic behind naming it the Palladion Project, which was primarily based upon Greek mythology. The Palladion was the name of the wooden statue that fell from heaven and was stored at Troy, safely protecting the city while they possessed it. Athena, the daughter of the sea-god Triton, accidentally killed her friend Pallas in a war game. While grieving her death, she fabricated this wooden statue in her likeness. I had also learned some interesting trivia about Athena. She was considered the goddess of wisdom and war, obtaining no pleasure from battle while preferring to settle conflict though mediation. So, I guessed that it was sensible for a survivability project to be named after a statue that protected an ancient city.

Before I started my long road trip to my new job on Friday, I attended an important meeting with the previous project manager. This was held immediately following my graduation. He told me that he wanted to see me before I departed. Fortunately, he was in town to attend my graduation ceremony. During the meeting, he was very talkative, and even meticulous when talking about the project. He even listed some of the critical issues that I was going to encounter when I start work on Monday. In my naïve judgment, I felt capable of overcoming these issues. Then, he said something that struck me as being very weird, to say the least. Handing me a small replica of the Palladion statue, he told me in a very authoritative and energetic voice what to do with it. I was on the verge of hysteria and about to laugh out loud since his instructions did not make any sense; but, I wrote them in my work journal anyways. This work journal was something that I had never used before. Yet, some of my project management instructors told me that this was useful. So, I began writing a record of anything of importance, which really helped me prepare for some of those difficult project management exams.

His instructions were simple, though. Whenever I needed help, I was to hold the statue in my hands while looking into a mirror. By trying to be considerate, I asked him what this meant, even though I could not believe his yarn of a tale. He replied that I would know when it happened. This was definitely weird. Nevertheless, I wrote this down, mostly to make him feel that I was listening to him, and partially to avoid laughing. I never thought that I would ever do anything like that though. Did he think that I was gullible and would do that? I expected Allen or Peter Funt to jump out telling me to "smile" – which did not happen. It took great restraint on my part to avoid asking him if I needed to recite an incantation too, such as "Mirror, Mirror, on the wall ..." Afterwards, I departed the school and began my two-day road trip to my new job, and my new apartment. And, to what would make a Twilight Zone episode seem normal.

First Premonition

A man who does not think and plan long ahead will find trouble right at his door.

Confucius, Chinese Ethical Teacher and Philosopher

It was Monday morning and I was excited about starting off on the right foot, especially making a good first impression. I drove to work early so that I would not be late, not knowing what the traffic was like. Luckily, I located a good parking spot. Then, I collected my things and walked to the front desk in the lobby. While signing in, the guard called someone to escort me. Because I was a new employee not having a security ID badge, I needed an escort. Security must be tight here. For a survivability project, I guessed that security was important.

My escort was a charming man who introduced himself as my administrative assistant. He was eagerly awaiting my arrival that morning and handed me an orientation folder containing some important information, such as names of key personnel and their telephone numbers. After escorting me to my new office to drop my things off, he provided me a quick tour of the building. It had to be quick since I had a busy day with a full schedule of events, beginning an hour after my early arrival. It was a good thing that I arrived early.

After the brief tour, I quickly unpacked. Among my things was that Palladion statue. I still did not know why I even bothered to bring that thing with me to work. Maybe I had an unconscious desire to see if it really did work. As instructed, I held the statue in my hands and looked into the mirror, which was located in my office. Nothing happened, just like I expected. Or, maybe I was supposed to have said an incantation. Oh well! I put the statue back on the desk and prepared for my first meeting.

Prior to the meeting, my assistant project manager entered my office and introduced himself, mentioning that he was a retired military officer. I was impressed that he had a successful military career. He continued talking, but I did not hear what he was saying since I was overly concerned that I did not have any military experience, especially when supporting a major DoD project. I ended the discussion and asked him to lead me to the conference room for the weekly project update meeting. On the way to the meeting, he handed me an important memo from my one of our key customers, a government product manager for military systems. I was told that I should read this before the meeting.

As I entered the conference room, I noticed it was definitely noisy, filled with several individual conversations. Then, the room quickly became quiet. I guessed that everyone noticed that someone new, me, had just entered their world. Before starting the meeting, I introduced myself to everyone stating that I was honored to be working on this important national defense project. I think that was what every new manager did. Also attending this meeting was the chief scientist, the lead engineer, the chief software developer, the chief maintenance technician, head of the HSE (health, safety, environmental) group, the chief accountant, a public outreach representative, and the military liaison officer. This was an impressive group of individuals. Unfortunately, I did not have time during the meeting to learn more about them. But, I would. A good manager always knew his people. At least that was what they told me in my project management course.

Just before sitting down and starting the meeting, I quickly read the memo. It stated our customer's desires. More specifically, it stated their displeasure with the project. In essence, they wanted reduced costs by 10%, removal of three months from the schedule for fielding of the first prototype item, and modification of our platform module making it installation capable in their entire current suite of military vehicles. This seemed reasonable. When two of the attendees provided their updates, they also included some important things that I needed to know. So, my response to their issues involved accommodating our customer.

The first was the chief accountant, who personally mentioned that there were some problems with the project schedule. This schedule did not contain all of the activities associated with the project, such as listing all meeting dates and the resources necessary to conduct those meetings. The key word in this was "ALL." I asked him what was needed to improve the schedule. His answer was a simple one. In his soft-spoken and unimaginative response, he stated that we needed more labor hours for our scheduling department. Knowing that we could not hire any additional schedulers, I suggested that he could use overtime to correct this problem.

The other person with issues was the chief software developer, who arrogantly indicated that he was behind schedule in finalizing the software development plan. He had been working on this plan for over a year now and was still obtaining useful improvement ideas that would make our system better. Being somewhat sarcastic and melodramatic in his discussion, he said that he wanted to visit one of the local software development companies in town to discuss ways to improve his plan. Because this was not going to cost me any additional money and because I did not want to begin a confrontation with one of my key people, I reluctantly agreed with him. I also told him that it was important for us to improve our plans, which was what I had learned during those mandatory performance improvement classes that I took. I still remembered learning about Drucker, Deming, and Ishikawa and their influence in improving business performance globally.

Finally, the meeting was over, hoping that no one noticed that I was very nervous, especially about avoiding the appearance of incompetence. Nevertheless, I felt good about myself. I made some good, yet easy, decisions today. I was now satisfying our customers, improving our schedules and improving our software plans. This was fun. It was even easier in real life than it was in class. Because I had time before my next meeting, I returned to my office to finish unpacking.

I accidentally glanced at my mirror in my office while I was moving that statue thing from my desk to the bookshelf. I noticed some ripples on the mirror surface. Not believing that I was seeing something, I rubbed my eyes and began staring at the mirror. Maybe, I was coming down with a headache. Or, maybe not. I continued looking at the mirror and the ripples persisted, which began to look like waves on the surface of a slightly calm lake. Then, the mirror image faded from a reflection of me to a foggy gray void. Then, something else began to appear. It started to become more focused with increased clarity. With the signal becoming stronger, this was like watching an ancient wireless TV, the ones with rabbit ears and the wireless signal coming directly from a local station several miles away. The image appearing was my conference room; and, I recognized the people in the room. Unlike a TV show, I was able to zoom in and out while panning around the room by thinking about it. It was similar to attending a meeting via video teleconference with no one knowing that I was there. This was cool! I questioned if it was real though.

These people appeared different. I also noticed a daily schedule, unconsciously zooming to it. I was startled after reading the date, which was four months into the future. Unlike the previous meeting I had just attended, this meeting occurring in my mirror was less jovial. The people appeared to be tired and upset. Mysteriously, my assistant project manager was chairing the meeting. What happened to me, I asked myself. Nervously, I soon found out.

The assistant project manager, who was now the acting project manager, started the meeting by saying that I had been reassigned back to corporate headquarters. I guessed that I was involuntarily removed from my position. More bluntly, I must have been fired. I did not even survive half of a year. No surprise there, after I heard the rest of the meeting.

During this meeting, I understood that my project was in serious jeopardy of defaulting on our defense contract.

Huh? My project was failing? I could not imagine what had happened. After observing this meeting a little longer, I also heard that our military client was definitely not happy with us. In my brilliant efforts to improve the performance of our system, our schedule had slipped several months, resulting in cost over-runs in excess of 15% of the budget. I thought that I was very clear in telling everyone that we needed to improve our schedule performance and reduce cost. It wasn't my fault. I also heard that we were still expending overtime hours to obtain an excellent schedule. However, no one was using that excellent schedule. In fact, they were reluctant to use it, especially since it was substantially complex and time-consuming to maintain. Finally, I heard that we were still improving our software development plan, even though we should have been fielding our product with the software already loaded. Once again, this was not my fault. Foolishly, I thought that the customer wanted a better product.

Then, the mirror began to fade, revealing my sweaty face. Silently, I began questioning myself if this happened because of my seemingly good decisions a few hours ago. I figured that I had better re-analyze and determine what could have gone wrong with what I had just decided.

Thinking about cost, schedule and performance, maybe we cannot have all three. I now remembered someone telling me about trade-space for making decisions. If we tried to improve all three, there would be no room for accomplishing those improvements. Maybe, I should have talked with the customer to determine what they really needed, including when they needed it. Now, for using a better schedule, expending resources to improve a tool that would not be used was not fiscally sound. Finally, improving a plan that would not be used was like throwing money away. While recovering from this insight of recognizing the problems of my previous actions, I wrote the following lessons into my work journal:

1. ***Cannot have all three: faster, better, cheaper.*** Although there are exceptions for innovative solutions, running a project with these three requirements results in no room for prioritization. Without the trade-space, complying with these three requirements usually results in un-desired costs somewhere.

2. ***Accomplishing the task is more important than the tools.*** Developing the best resource-loaded schedule that is not used is wasteful. The customers

do not need to know what tools you used; instead, they are more concerned with the product end-state performance.

3. ***Plan and sacrifice now for the sake of the future.*** Expending overtime and other resources to obtain near-term requirements was the same as expending future dollars, leaving less funding to complete the project. Decisions should be made to optimize the use of resources for both short and long term requirements.

4. ***A poor plan implemented is much better than the best plan that is not implemented.*** Spending years to develop the best plan for implementing the project that needed to be completed in a few months is a failure. Someone else could beat you to market.

I wondered if other successful managers learned about being a better manager through visions just like Abraham Lincoln's dream of his death hours before his assassination, Otto von Bismarck's prediction of the First World War starting in the Balkans, and Nostradamus's predictions. Nobly, I felt good about being in good company if I could view the future like these three eminent gentlemen.

Second Premonition

Information's pretty thin stuff unless mixed with experience.

Clarence Day, American Essayist

After surviving that first day on the job, I was still trying to determine if that premonition from yesterday was real or not. Impulsively, I tried several times to hold the statue and look in the mirror. Unfortunately, nothing happened. Maybe it was just my imagination. In fact, maybe it really was a headache causing me to have a day dream. In any event, the four lessons that I wrote in my diary were still beneficial. I applied those lessons, making changes on my project to ensure successful completion in the future.

Because of the limited project resources and the need to put something in the field quickly, I asked my technical experts to consider trading some of the performance requirements for speed and cost. In additional meetings, I tactfully convinced my project personnel to prioritize product performance with less emphasis upon the tools used. I also considered future ramifications resulting from my decisions. Finally, I ensured that we did not "spin our wheels" trying to improve everything while accomplishing nothing. With these changes implemented, I was very confident that this project was going to succeed. I was even happy about it.

This second day was going to be another long one, as this was the day of our project's quarterly management review. The previous project manager implemented this review process about six months ago. However, since the last update, each of my subordinate organizations developed many metrics to be included in this review, which eventually grew to a six-hour meeting discussing 138 separate metrics. These metrics were grouped into the following areas: safety, environmental, funding, schedules, personnel, performance, engineering, testing, procurement, marketing, customer satisfaction, and upcoming events. I could not believe that anything was missing from this colossal set of metrics. Sarcastically, I was thinking that the only metric we were missing was the tracking of parking lot etiquette violations. I really wanted to ask someone during the meeting about that, but fortunately kept my mouth closed.

———————

During this metrics review meeting, I asked for the assumptions supporting the metrics, knowing that these affected the data being presented. From this list, I perceptively grouped them into four areas of assumptions. First one involved resources: personnel with the right skills would be available; hardware resources would be available; access to experts with specialized skills would be available; and, full-time personnel productivity would be at least 36 hours effective work per week. Next one was generic: no testing or manufacturing action would be taken that would affect the project; issues would be resolved in a timely manner; and, systems components would be capable of being integrated with minimum rework. Third one involved the budget: information used in preparing the estimates would be accurate to within 5%, and no outside consulting would be required. Final set of assumptions involved functionality: the scope of work for the project would not change, and formal charter and scope change procedures would be followed. These all sounded like someone meticulously developed valid assumptions. I wondered if they were really valid though. I erroneously guessed that it did not matter since these all professionals who should be cognizant of valid and realistic assumptions used on previously used metrics.

As the data was presented, I was concerned that we all did not really understand what the data meant. But, no one else was questioning the data; so, I kept quiet. Later in the meeting, during one of the many boring discussions, I had a flashback to one of my project management professors illustrating this lack of understating using the paradox of percentages. This paradox involved a bag containing 100 steel balls, both small and large. Three different people were asked to calculate the percentage of large balls in this bag with each providing contradictory results: 1%, 50%, and 99%. I originally thought that two of these had to be wrong. Authoritatively, the professor continued discussing the paradox by stating that all three answers were correct. No way!! When I first heard this, I thought about nominating him for the fictional absent-minded professor of the year award. Even though I was becoming flustered, I continued hearing this professor state that the first person was an accountant concerned with the number of balls – 1 large and 99 small, resulting in 1% by number. I thought that this must be the real correct answer, with the other two definitely being wrong. The second person was a painter concerned with the surface area of the balls involving the amount of paint to procure – the 1 large ball had a surface area of about 600 in^2 and the total amount of the surface area of the very small 99 balls had the same cummulative surface area, resulting in 50% by area. This must be a trick question. Finally, the third person was a truck driver concerned with the weight of the balls – the 1 large ball weighing about 396 pounds and all of the 99 small balls together weighing about 4 pounds, resulting in 99% by weight. I could not believe this. I would have made a different decision depending upon which percentage I had heard. No wonder people hate numbers so much.

I thought to myself that I should stop reminiscing about my project management lessons and pay attention to what was being discussed. Throughout the entire six hours of discussing the numerous eye-charts, I asked several questions to give the appearance that I was really listening to them, even though I did not understand much of it. After deciding the date and location of the next quarterly metrics meeting, the meeting was over. Whew! I pondered what else I had to accomplish before I departed for the day.

After returning to my office, I stared at that statue thing, thinking that it may work again. With nothing to lose, I grabbed it and looked at the mirror. Nothing. I did not really think it would actually work. As I was returning the

---

statue back to the bookshelf, I glanced at the mirror and noticed the ripples again. Uh oh! I guessed that it was about to happen again. Through some unseen force drawing me to the mirror, I willingly drew closer to the mirror, waiting until it cleared up again.

This time, I was seeing frustrated people yelling on the production floor at our test facility, wondering why they were yelling. As I continued to watch the scene in the mirror, I understood, seeing an ambulance arrive and transport an injured employee to the hospital. One of the employees condescendingly told her supervisor that this should not have happened, indicating that the first aid and near miss data available should have alerted someone to potential safety-related problems in the plant. Then, the mirror began to ripple. I guessed that this was all that I was going to see; until I saw something other than my face appear in the mirror.

Now, I was observing a shift change meeting in the same test facility. It did not look like the same day as the accident in the previous vision. During this meeting, I overheard several of the employees arguing that management did not know what was going on in the plant.

In their rebellious arguments, they pointed to several graphs on the wall, which were some of the same ones presented to me in the quarterly meeting earlier that day. They must have had some problems with these metrics. Listening to them, I discovered what those problems were. One of the graphs listed the assumptions. Apparently, the project was having issues obtaining people with the right skills, avoiding unnecessary testing, maintaining an unchanging budget estimate, and avoiding scope creep. I guessed that our assumptions were not valid at all. Maybe, I should have validated those assumptions.

Then, another image appeared in the mirror. Already exhausted, I quietly asked myself how many of these I was going to experience. In this one, I observed another shift change meeting with different people laughing at some of the graphs on the wall. I guessed that there were other problems with these metrics. The chief maintenance technician was the primary talkative person in this vision. He was very good at trouble-shooting our production equipment by using his extensive experience along with his recent associate's degree in mechanical technology from the local community college. I quickly determined that others listening to him took his comments seriously.

During this vision, this perceptive technician passionately and inquisitively questioned why management was solely concerned about measuring the amount of work being done, such as hours expended and lines of software code being developed. Being melodramatic, he answered his own question by stating that it was to track how busy we were. Flustered, he suggested that management could generate several long meetings each day to discuss work, recording these meetings as hours expended and making their metrics appear good. He also suggested that we develop computer programs using inefficient coding, which involves a computer programmer writing several lines of code when only one line would accomplish the same. Hmm! Maybe, our metrics were focused upon tracking how busy we were and not assessing what our customer really wanted, which was a product that did what the customer wanted, when they wanted it, and expended the least amount of resources. Then, again, why did we spend a lot of time talking about metrics, doing nothing with them? With all of the money wasted developing, implementing, maintaining, and discussing metrics, there should have been some benefit to the project.

As the mirror faded back to the present, I found myself reminiscing again about another lecture I heard in my project management course. The instructor indicated that all manufacturing processes were extremely complicated, with thousands of variables intertwined with one another. Actions to improve one variable may occur at the expense of another. In essence, there were a few overall performance metrics that really indicated what was happening: cost, cycle time, safety, and quality. Most of the other variables, or performance metrics, supported these overall ones. Considering this, I spent the next several hours developing the key metrics to gauge the performance on my project. I reduced our 138 metrics down to the "dirty dozen." I wanted to have a catchy phrase, such as linking it to that 1967 Lee Marvin movie about a group of misfit Soldiers assigned to accomplish an impossible mission. All other metrics could be used in support of these. Prior to leaving for the day to obtain some needed sleep, I wrote the following four lessons that I learned into my journal.

5. *Metrics should be used if you plan to use them for decisions.* Tracking safety statistics without using them to make safety-related decisions was the same

as not using the metric. This was true for all other metrics too.

6. ***Understand the source of the data.*** The decision to install insulation based upon temperature gauge readings during testing could be flawed if one did not know if the temperature probes were in the correct location providing correct measurements. This was similar to the expression of "garbage in, garbage out." We needed to ensure that we did not have "garbage" in our measurements.

7. ***Meaningless goals, even if they are easy to obtain, should not be used.*** Having a goal to track the expenditure of 500 hours of work was easier to track than measuring the performance of that work. Measuring performance usually resulted in improving performance. However, one should choose the final performance that one wanted improved, such as quantity of units produces instead of the quantity of employees trained that would be necessary to produce the desired units.

8. ***Challenge Your Assumptions (CYA).*** Assumptions may be easy to state, especially when used to support preconceived ideas. However, all

assumptions should be verified continually for validity and applicability.

I hoped tomorrow would be a better day. Now to get some sleep. I better not have any dreams tonight, especially not nightmares. These day visions were definitely draining.

Third Premonition

We hold the view that the people make the best judgment in the long run.

John F. Kennedy, 35th US President

In my office after quickly scanning my inbox of new e-mail, I reflected upon the difficulties of actually being the project manager. It looked so easy when I was watching someone do it. I did not realize how difficult it would become. After learning about the tools taught to me in my project management courses, I thought it was going to be easy. However, it appeared that every little thing that I did had a tremendous impact upon performance of the project. With this in mind, I had hoped that I did not mess up too much today. Today was the day that I visit other members of my team at two of our remote locations. Fortunately, they were located not too far away and within driving distance.

I met our lead design engineer at the first site, where the design of the sensors for the project was performed. She supervised four other multi-disciplined engineers who were involved in this design. Prior to this meeting, I took the fortunate opportunity to read her personnel file, learning that she possessed two master's degrees, one in electrical engineering from a nationally well-known university and an executive one in business management from the nearby state university. Before she worked on this project, she worked for a major national construction firm involved in a wide variety of facility construction systems. I also discovered that she was very innovative, willing to "think outside of the box;" which I deduced after reading about her patent of a novel remote sensor-based discriminative detection system. Also looking at her previous evaluations, I determined that she was a hard worker, normally accomplishing whatever given her. She definitely had a spotless record. I was glad that she worked for me.

During this meeting, she energetically presented me with the status of the current sensor design effort. Her group developed robust equipment for both passive and active threat detection. During the subsequent discussions, she talked about the technical issues, which primarily involved wireless bands using acronyms such as NIR, IR, RF and others that I was not too familiar. While encouraging me about the ultimate performance of this system, she mentioned that the current design involved the development of multiple-use sensors using multi-spectrum systems – whatever that meant. Not knowing what to ask, I returned to the basic sensor functions, asking about the different threat detections that were being considered. She further indicated that the ground-based threats such as mines detection were her primary focus. However, she added that the air-based threats such as in-flight munitions were also being developed. I concluded the meeting by inquiring whether environmental sensors such as weather conditions were being designed. Hesitantly, she responded by stating that another vendor was providing that with off-the-shelf sensors.

At the second site, I met our chief scientist, who was very eager to discuss the upcoming tests on Saturday. His demeanor reminded me of the typical absented-minded college professor who was very interested in discovering new things, not caring about how the rest of the world was functioning. Arrogantly, he presented me with lots of data and graphs, providing his interpretation of what he thought that it meant. He even discussed his innovative methodology for developing numerical solutions to complex, non-linear, partial differential equations using large-scale computational algorithms. This definitely went over my head! This was never discussed in any math course that I ever took. Wanting to visit his people and tour the laboratory, I quickly changed the topic by asking him to show me his facilities. While walking from one room to another, each filled with electrical gadgets and other analytical devices, he clumsily introduced me to several of his colleagues. This was all very fascinating, yet slightly intimidating. It further amazed me how anyone could obtain useful data from this complicated and seemly messy setup.

This completed my off-site tours, successfully allowing me to visit my facilities and meet some of the workers. Now for my drive back to the office. While driving, I was pondering what I would learn from that statue thing. I could not wait, even though I could not imagine what I could have done wrong during my visits. After returning, I quickly retrieved the statue and headed towards the mirror. I eagerly wanted to know what my decisions that day caused, if any.

Then it happened. The mirror began to fade, meaning that I must have done something wrong again. Oh well.

These visionary experiences did help me correct previous situations before they became disasters. The mirror displayed the image of the engineering war room, located at the first site I visited earlier in the day. In this vision, I observed the lead engineer angrily discussing issues with her other engineers. One of the other engineers complained that the project manager (me) did not appreciate his work. He substantiated his comments with my response to his personal presentation to me. Apparently, the data in his presentation were very significant, resulting from his consistent dedication and effort in obtaining it. I guessed that I had upset him with my unenthusiastic response of asking him if this effort could have been improved by using a new software program that was in a recent project management magazine. Apparently, he wanted me to recognize his effort. I wondered why the lead engineer did not provide me a "heads up" for this.

Another engineer discussed another recurring burning issue in this meeting. A couple of months ago, another engineer in the company boldly plagiarized his work by taking credit for an innovative design proposal he developed for another of our key clients. When he brought this issue to management's attention, nothing happened. At least, that was the perception by these engineers. The plagiarizing engineer still worked on the project; and, no praise was bestowed upon the real innovative engineer, who just blatantly indicated in this meeting that he was aggressively looking for another job with an employer who treated their employees with respect. I remembered reading about this issue in my long stack of files on my desk. Maybe, I should dig into this issue further and correct any wrong-doings.

Then, the mirror began transforming into another image, that of a laboratory. In this vision, one of the scientists was commenting that the person in charge was incompetent. The chief scientist, normally managing the laboratory, departed on an un-expectant business trip to meet a client to discuss their project scope changes. The next senior person in the laboratory was delegated to be in charge during this chief scientist's absence, expected to last about a week. It was obvious that this person did not know anything about running a laboratory, let alone supervising others. He may have been a competent scientist; but, he did not know how to lead or manage people. I realized this when I saw him agree with someone's concerns, contradicting one of his previous decisions. For example, he impulsively agreed that the analytical chemist could initiate an extensive literature research and postpone conducting analytical measurements of the ongoing experiments until tomorrow. This was followed by him nonchalantly agreeing with the metallurgist that the analytic chemist should conduct more analytical measurements so that the results of the experiments can be finished early. This would provide the metallurgist with the data he needed. It was apparent that the senior scientist did not know what the actual priorities were. Come to think about it, I did not know what the priorities were; so, how could the rest of the people on the project? Also, I had better look at a succession plan within the project to ensure continuity of leadership during the absence of my key leaders.

The mirror faded back to normal. This time, most of what I observed in the mirror was not a result of my direct decision. Instead, some of these problems were traced back to the previous project manager. However, these were still problems that I could and should resolve quickly.

Otherwise, I would be the cause of those failures through my inactions. Beginning tomorrow, I would do just that. However, before I forgot, I needed to capture what I had learned from the mirror. The following were my next four lessons.

9. ***A project begins, ends, fails, and succeeds with people.*** Projects were run by people and managed by people, not machines. As such, project related decisions should account for the human factor.

10. ***Reward good performers; coach or remove bad ones.*** Accountability gives others expectations on their performance including proving them motivation. Without this accountability, there would be no way to ensure that your decisions are implemented.

11. ***Train your successor.*** When not in the office, such as for vacation or on a business trip, you should have someone capable of doing your tasks; otherwise, there will be no one capable of replacing you.

12. ***Do not try to please everyone; someone will not like it.*** Not everyone would be pleased about the working hours or the people they worked with. Decisions should be based upon the optimal

solution, not trying to satisfy the needs or wants of everybody.

These premonitional lessons were definitely making me wise, at least in my mind. Maybe, I should consider teaching project management to others. But first, I needed to manage this project, since I had almost completed the first week. This list was obviously becoming bigger, though. I silently questioned why no one had told me about these before. I guessed that I had to experience it myself, just like kids not believing their parents. Oh, that reminded me that I had better call my mom tonight.

———————

Fourth Premonition

You people are telling me what you think I want to know. I want to know what is actually happening.

General Creighton Abrams, US Commander in
Vietnam from 1968 - 1972

As I walked to my office, I realized that the week was more than half gone. I survived three days in charge of this project, with about a thousand more left. You could say one thing about this job, it never became boring. Well, at least until today, with multiple meetings, back-to-back to attend this day. According to this schedule, my last meeting of the day did not end until after 9 pm. I wondered if we had time to eat lunch and dinner, especially since there was no time in my schedule for those. Just in case, I decided to put a couple of bags of peanuts, the unopened ones I still had from previous air trips, into my briefcase.

My first scheduled meeting was another weekly project status meeting – I thought that I had attended one of these weekly meetings on Monday. I thought that this was going to be a quick meeting; but, we discussed every little problem or issue on the project, including hearing everyone's opinion about them. This was nothing more than a free-for-all meeting with no discipline. I guessed that was how they conducted meetings on this project. During this meeting, our most experienced design engineer pointed out that we had data indicating that there were still electrical and instrumentation errors with the sensor. He strongly recommended that we postpone the test until these problems were resolved.

Knowing that I wanted other opinions, I asked for the ideas and thoughts of the other people in the meeting. One of our less experienced engineers optimistically mentioned that he was systematically working on this issue and would probably fix it before Saturday. Other people in the meeting, especially the non-engineer and non-technical ones voted that we should still conduct the test, even without the problems completely resolved. I concurred, since we had a majority of the people in the meeting agree with this course of action. However, in the back of my mind, I knew that there was no assurance or guarantee that they would accomplish this. Also thinking to myself, I considered informing the corporate office to postpone the test on Saturday until we resolved this issue.

Unfortunately, I assumed that my boss did not want to hear any potential bad news; so, I kept this information to myself. This meeting lasted until early afternoon. No lunch. Good thing that I packed those peanuts. I was hungry.

My next meeting was with the Test & Evaluation Working-level Integrated Project Team (WIPT). This was a critical meeting for the project's testing program, especially with the Preliminary Production Qualification Test scheduled for Saturday. This was our company's practice test prior to the Government's Production Qualification Test (PQT), which was a key milestone used by them to validate our design and manufacturing processes. We needed to be successful on this PQT, which was needed to successfully complete the developmental phase of the project and continue into the operational phase. Also, a monetary performance incentive was tied to successful completion of this milestone before the end of this month. So, I had expected several corporate executives observing this test on Saturday. My boss was on the phone during this teleconference meeting and asked if everything for the test was ready, to which I had elusively responded that we had no problems, implying that this test should be successful. This meeting adjourned just before 7 pm, leaving me just a few minutes to make my next meeting. And satisfying my hunger pains, to stop by the vending machines for one of those stale sandwiches. Next time, I will bring lunch with me.

My last meeting was the monthly stakeholder's forum. Earlier, I did not know why there was a meeting scheduled this late in the day. However during the meeting, I found out why. This was a teleconference meeting with key individuals from other parts of the world, primarily located in the Asia Pacific basin area. There, the day was just beginning. I quickly learned that being the project manager of a global project also meant being responsible for talking with others around the world. The purpose of this meeting was to discuss the current project status with emphasis upon future activities. It was a quick two-hour meeting with not much being decided. Nevertheless, it was still late, but I felt compelled again to use that statue thing to determine if there was something I could have done to improve upon today's activities. I could not have imagined that it would be too much, since I felt good about the three meetings earlier. Oh my, was I ever wrong!

———

As the mirror became clearer, I saw our test facility. It was Saturday, the day of that important test. I eagerly waited to see what the results on Saturday were going to be. I watched as the vehicle test platform, mounted with our sensor device, was moving down the road. It was definitely quiet, with everyone's attention watching the vehicle move. This first of three tests was to validate that the sensor would be able to detect a landmine from a distance of five meters. This should work, since I saw the data myself; and, most people in the WIPT meeting agreed with this. Not all, but most did agree if I remember correctly. After a few minutes, I saw the test vehicle drive over the landmine without any indication of it. It failed. This should not have happened.

Good thing that this was just a preliminary test. Several of the design engineers noisily worked on trying to fix the sensors on the vehicle. Now, they were going to try it again. Being frustrated in my observations, I saw the vehicle drive by the mines without detection. And, we tried it again, and again, each time failing to detect the mines. Oh no, I did not want to see what was going to happen next. As anticipated, my boss was very upset and went straight to the design engineers to ask what went wrong.

One of the engineers calmly mentioned that we knew about this problem, wondering why he did not know. Oops! Maybe, I should have informed my boss. Boy, did I ever feel incompetent. Come to think of it, I still had time to tell him before Saturday.

Oh wait. The image did not disappear. There I was defensively explaining this situation to my boss. In this imagine, I was telling him how bad this situation was and explained the poor performance of others. I continued by explaining that this design was poorly fabricated and happened before I took over as the project manager earlier that week. It appeared that all I did was explain all of the bad items on the project in an effort to shift blame from me to others. My boss told me to stop talking and said that the whole project was a disaster of mammoth proportions and should be cancelled, which is what he was going to recommend to the corporate Board of Directors on Monday. And, he left before I could inform him about the good things that were being done on the project. Then, the image faded back to the present.

Now that it was Thursday evening in the present again, I decided that I had better talk to my boss. After sending him an e-mail explaining some of the issues that needed to be resolved before Saturday's test along with a list of all of the positive accomplishments, I called his phone number, leaving a voice message asking that he call me first thing the next morning to discuss these issues.

The problems in the first meeting that day reminded me of a book that I had read in my high school English class. The problem involved Groupthink, which I understood was intended to be similar to the Orwellian Newspeak words in the book **Nineteen Eighty-Four**. This represented the decisions by group members who tried to avoid conflict by reaching a consensus decision without critical analysis. In other words, these groups made hasty and irrational decisions out of fear of upsetting the harmony within the group. I guessed that I was guilty of this behavior today – I had better be more careful in future meetings. Now, I was ready to call it a day; but, I had to record another set of lessons that would even further improve my ability to lead this project.

13. *Consensus usually results in "weakest denominator" decisions.* For technical decisions, failure could be expected from making decisions

based upon a non-expert while disregarding a world-renown expert. This would be similar to asking a high-school dropout what to do during brain surgery.

14. ***Meetings should be short, infrequent, and value-added.*** Meetings with no actions are the same as wasting resources. A person's time was very important; so, wasting it in a meeting would not be wise.

15. ***Communicate the information, both good with the bad.*** Failure to communicate any type of information, both up and down the management chain, tended to cause poor decisions. Furthermore, one should not filter out certain information, especially for those making decisions.

16. ***Sell the good statements, not the bad, even though it is easier for the bad ones.*** Frequently communicating bad information usually resulted in the organization having a bad performance culture and bad reputation. No one wanted to work for or with a bad organization, as people wanted to be on the winning team.

As I wrote these in my journal, I wondered if anyone else was having these strange premonitions, or prophecies of the future. I better not tell anyone. As Josh Billings, a 19th Century US Lecturer, once said, *"Don't ever prophesy; for if you prophesy wrong, nobody will forget it; and if you prophesy right, nobody will remember it."*

Fifth Premonition

The chief cause of problems is solutions.

Eric Sevareid, American Broadcast Journalist

After entering my office on this bright Friday morning, just one day before the important test, I noticed that the red light was blinking on my phone. This indicated that I had a voice message. I immediately listened to it, assuming it was a response to my voice message to my boss the night before about some technical problems with the sensors. My assumption proved to be correct. It was my boss in his Southern-style charming voice explaining to me that he was sending a corporate engineering expert to the manufacturing facility in the morning to help troubleshoot the problems. He strongly suggested that I personally observe these activities. Since this site was a few hours away, I decided to drive there immediately after I finished scanning, my e-mail.

The manufacturing facility was the primary location where we were building and testing the sensors. It was located in an abandoned warehouse in a small town that used to be home to several large industrial plants. However, with the strong global competition, these plants were not successful in maintaining their original market share. This was mostly the result of not continuing to improve upon their previous successes. I read a recent historical account of this explaining that during the 1970's, these plants were very successful. However, during the 1980s and early 1990s, they neglected to update their manufacturing methods to incorporate new technologies, especially informational technologies. Their philosophy was "if it ain't broke, don't fix it." So, they did not change, allowing their competitors to surpass them. I guessed that this common philosophy was a fatal flaw.

After arriving, I quickly located the engineers to get their progress report. They were finishing some diagnostic tests to determine if some of the parts were problematic. A few minutes later, in several triumphant voices, they told me that they found a faulty part that caused the problem. My project engineer originally assumed that the parts were faultless, believing that the vendor provided only working parts. I inquired into which part was faulty. The answer I received did not make sense, but did resolve the problem.

Apparently, one of the clamps holding the sensor in place did not work. More specifically, the red-colored clamps had a defect that caused it to crack prematurely, thus causing the sensor to pop out of the socket. However, the green-colored clamps used in the original testing from the same vendor worked. So, after replacing all of the red clamps with the green ones and successfully re-testing the sensors again, all five of the sensors being used for the test on Saturday should work. With this in mind, I signed a product specification directive dictating that only green-colored clamps can be used for our sensors. This was easy. Now I had time for more work back at the office.

I returned to the office that afternoon, more confident that the test for Saturday was going to be successful. I bet that my boss was going to be happy. After attempting to log into my computer unsuccessfully, I discovered that the information technology group was upgrading everyone's computer with new software. Being concerned about this, I asked them what computer software program was being loaded, being told that it was a new project scheduling program. I then asked for their schedule for future software uploads or upgrades, finding out that they do this when needed, which was about once every three or four months.

_____

However, these IT professionals wanted to globally update all project computers for several hours every Friday afternoon. I asked why, being told that they wanted to do this to stay ahead of all technology improvements. Not wanting to suffer the same consequences of those industrial plants that failed to embrace informational technologies, I agreed that this was a good thing, and asked them to begin doing this next week.

After finally reading everything in my inbox, I noticed that it was dark outside, meaning that the normal work day was over. As I did every day that week, I took the statue to that enchanting mirror for some professional self improvement. The image that appeared was like none of the others. It consisted of several military officers located in a remote war-torn village sometime in the distant future. These officers were complaining about the continual failures of their vehicles' sensors to detect mines, resulting in numerous fatalities. The primary cause of these failures was linked to one part, the clamp holding the sensor in place. I thought that this could not be true, since we solved that problem this morning by eliminating red clamps. These officers were reading my memo directing that only green clamps be used, resulting in their uncontrolled laughter. They were questioning my professional competence by asking themselves how I could have suspected color had anything to do with this material of construction problem.

I guessed that I fell into the trap of a formal fallacy, more specifically a false dilemma. I remembered from my project management training that this type of dilemma usually involved two alternatives which were often extreme ones. An example of this would be, "you are either with us or against us," which discounted any other type of position. On my project, the dilemma was green versus red color parts. This was also like the classic story of the blind men and an elephant, used to demonstrate that reality could be viewed differently depending upon one's perspective. In this story, six blind men concluded that the elephant was either a wall, a snake, a spear, a tree, a fan, or a rope, depending upon where they touched. I decided to direct my engineers to look into this again and determine a different and better root cause of this problem.

The proven industrial process for resolving problems usually began with determining the real root cause, such as using the "5 whys" process. I remembered one of my project management instructors illustrating this through the "dark room" analogy. This involved the identification of a problem developed after walking into a dark room. The following table illustrated the typical type of questions that could be asked, each developed from the answer to the previous question.

Question	Answer
Why was the room dark?	*The lamp did not work.*
Why did the lamp not work?	*The light bulb did not work.*
Why did the bulb not work?	*Was no power to the lamp.*
Why was there no power?	*The light switch was not on.*
Why was the light switch off?	*Cannot find the light switch.*
Why can't you find the switch?	*The light switch was in the back of the closet on the far end of the room, per engineering design.*

In this analogy, the real cause for the room being dark was poor engineering of the light switch location. The other five reasons were really symptoms, resulting in the better solution to this problem by correcting the engineering design. If changing the design could not be done, which may happen for many engineering related problems, then the solution would be to compensate for the inadequacies of the design by revising how the people used the system. This could be training people about the unusual location of the light switch in this example.

The next image that appeared in the mirror was of my office center. There were several project employees discussing the problems they had with their computers. From their heated discussions, I quickly learned that they were unable to perform their work. In fact, the new software continually being installed on their computers had the adverse effect upon the employees, with them being incapable of using the new changes, mostly as a result of the immense training required. Apparently, each new upgrade or installation required about two full days of training for employees to understand the system effectively. Hearing this, I immediately calculated this in my head, which translated to a 40% decrease in productivity. Although these improvements kept my office on the leading edge of technology, this solution was more costly than using older technology. Maybe, this was how solutions or IT changes in the past were done; today, we needed a better solution by controlling which technologies we needed to use.

Then the image returned back to the present, with my sweaty concerned face peering back at me – again. Being patriotic and concerned about fatalities, I modified my direction for green-only clamps and directed that a root-cause investigation be conducted to determine the real problem. I also drafted another office memo to the IT department directing that any future upgrades or additions be justified and approved by me before implementation. Afterwards, I began to write in my journal.

17. ***Today's problems come from yesterday's solutions.*** Using old technology and knowledge may not be enough to solve the problem. This may even duplicate the problem.
18. ***The cure can be worse than the disease.*** Spending 100 hours solving a problem to save 10 hours was the same as wasting 90 hours.
19. ***Dominate technology; do not let it dominate you.*** This was like having new software to change the way we work, such as using mass-mailings of e-

mail to improve your ability to micromanage. Instead, you should use new software to improve the way you work.

20. ***Solve the problem, not the symptom.*** Conducting a thorough "root cause" determination is necessary for effectively understanding the problem. For example, the manager should not be hasty in jumping to the wrong conclusion.

After another set of lessons developed from this premonition, I felt this project becoming more successful. I asked myself if I ever needed to buy another journal or take another project management course if I continued to learn more, especially practical lessons, with this statue. Still, I was nervous about the test the next morning, hoping that I would be able to sleep tonight.

Sixth Premonition

Nothing is more difficult, and therefore more precious, than to be able to decide.

Napoleon Bonaparte, French Emperor

Today was the day of the big test. Instead of going straight to my office, I went to the test facility located on a nearby defense department installation. Prior to the test, I personally inspected each vehicle to verify that the green clamp was being used. Even with a good night's sleep, I was still nervous. As anticipated, all five vehicle tests were successful in detecting the mines. Since there was some time remaining in the morning, our team met to begin developing a test plan for detection of aerial threats, such as missiles and projectiles. After this brief discussion, I dismissed everyone except for the engineers and testing professionals. I had made an appointment at the clamp equipment vendor to investigate why the green ones work instead of the red ones. I had also asked our materials scientist to attend this meeting.

After lunch, we had a brief meeting with the vendor to discuss our issues, providing them the results of our initial investigation. Writing on the whiteboard, one of our engineers developed a list of the commonalities and differences between the green and red clamps. We considered the raw materials, production dates, and production equipment. Other than the difference in color pigments used, these clamps were produced on different machines. We did not know why different machines could produce seemingly similar products with different characteristics; but, we decided to find out.

Following a quick safety briefing and issuance of safety protective equipment such as helmets and ear plugs, the vendor's production chief provided us a tour of their facility. This was very fascinating, since I had never seen a plastics injection molding machine before. The machine that we saw was producing a product similar to the clamps that we purchased for our sensors. This product was also made from nylon. During the tour, the production chief told us that the most important part of this machine was the mold, which consisted of two parts, called the core and the cavity. She further explained the injection process, which began with the mold closure followed by the heated plastic injected into it. After cooling the mold to solidify the plastic, the mold is opened to eject the part.

This was all fascinating, but I inquired into the typical problems for this process. After hearing typical problems such as short shots, flashes, jetting, and blistering, I was confused. This was all foreign to me. I must have slept through that chemistry lecture in college. So, I had better read more about plastic manufacturing if I was going to be working with plastics, especially being concerned about their defects. Returning back to the current issue, I asked them what potential problems that we had, showing them both the red and green clamps that we brought with us. After several minutes, one of the vendor engineers noticed some air pockets in the red clamp and suggested that we had a problem with voids, which usually occurs from a lack of a holding pressure in the injection molding machine. Whatever that meant. After everyone else saw these air pockets, we concluded that we discovered the root cause of the problem. With this discovery, we drafted a solution to resolve this problem.   We agreed that the vendor would update their production processes to ensure that the required production parameters were used; and, our acceptance criteria for these parts would include a visual investigation for these voids.

Now, it was time to return to the office and close out the paperwork for the tests, along with documenting our manufacturing visit with a trip report. After completing this, I was being lured back to the mirror. With the statue in hand again, I saw the mirror fade into another image, which was of another meeting of project personnel and customers discussing the sensors and why it was expensive and why it was not capable of being modified to detect non-metallic mines. Oh my! I had not considered changes of technologies and the need for changing our product. I was more focused upon ensuring that we continued doing things right forever. I never thought about doing the right thing, even if it was not done correctly every time.

This reminded me of the classic business school analogy of the buggy whip. With the advent of the automobile, the buggy whip manufacturers continued to act as if they were only in the buggy whip business. They focused upon doing things right, even reducing the prices of their whips. However, with the cars replacing horses for transportation, things changed. The external business environment, containing transportation customers, did not want these whips. But if they would have defined themselves as being in the "acceleration" business, they would have been able to support the automobile industry and have survived, instead of going out of business. Because I did not want to become a "buggy whip" project manager, I decided to re-look at the function that my project was selling, instead of focusing primarily upon the hardware.

The next vision was of the vendor's manufacturing process where I saw the engineers and production personnel trying to mold their product to the exact specifications that we provided them, including ensuring that they try to make things better. Since the raw materials and other production process had changed, using the older technologies for manufacturing required the vendor to maintain the injection molding equipment that was not supported by the molding vendors. This resulted in increased costs for the clamps, which could not be made anywhere else. Also, they were continually improving their equipment to provide enhancements that we really did not need, also increasing the cost of the part. I had better re-think about the concept of always trying to become better.

If I kept waiting until I obtained something better, I would never get anything accomplished; or, I would get something that I did not need.

Then, the image in the mirror returned to the present. Whew! This was a very tiring week, along with some soul-searching from the mirror. After considering what I had seen in this vision, I wrote some action items in my to-do list for next week. Among them was the need to assess our primary mission and develop processes to provide the customer with that function, even long after we completed the final fielding of the end item. After completing this to-do list, I wrote another four lessons into my book.

21. ***Doing the right thing is better than doing things right.*** Using the best process for using an ancient type-writer today may not be the best thing to do if you have access to computers.

22. ***Better is the enemy of good enough.*** Buying the best computer today and using it is better than waiting next year for a better computer. While you are waiting, you would not have the best computer to use today.

---

23. ***Resources mean nothing if not used.*** Having people on the project doing nothing productive has the same results of not having those people at all.

24. ***If it "ain't broke," either maintain or improve it.*** Doing nothing resulted in a reactive management while waiting for it to fail before doing something. Breaking it resulted in a repair mentality. Maintaining it meant using it and keeping it available for use.

I wondered if I would have these visions next week too. However, I did not think about work on Sunday, needing a much-deserved day of rest. As I was just about to power-down my computer, a new e-mail popped up. This was from a close friend of mine. In fact, this friend was my roommate in college and currently worked as a production supervisor in a local telecommunications company. I was invited to Sunday brunch, providing me an opportunity to discuss my interesting first week as a project manager, and my twenty-four project management lessons. Reading the e-mail further for more details, she mentioned that she was going to show me a picture of the bridesmaid dress that I was going to wear at her upcoming wedding. After confirming this brunch appointment and departing my office, I thought about …

Haraburda Project Management Rules

1. Cannot have all three: faster, better, cheaper.
2. Accomplishing the task is more important than the tools.
3. Plan and sacrifice now for the sake of the future.
4. A poor plan implemented is much better than the best plan that is not implemented.
5. Metrics should be used if you plan to use them for decisions.
6. Understand the source of the data.
7. Meaningless goals, even if they are easy to obtain, should not be used.
8. Challenge Your Assumptions (CYA).
9. A project begins, ends, fails, and succeeds with people.
10. Reward good performers; coach or remove bad ones.
11. Train your successor.
12. Do not try to please everyone; someone will not like it.
13. Consensus usually results in "weakest denominator" decisions.
14. Meetings should be short, infrequent, and value-added.
15. Communicate the information, both good with the bad.
16. Sell the good statements, not the bad, even though it is easier for the bad ones.
17. Today's problems come from yesterday's solutions.
18. The cure can be worse than the disease.
19. Dominate technology; do not let it dominate you.
20. Solve the problem, not the symptom.
21. Doing the right thing is better than doing things right.
22. Better is the enemy of good enough.
23. Resources mean nothing if not used.
24. If it "ain't broke," either maintain or improve it.

Author Bio

 Scott S. Haraburda is a Colonel who has served over twenty-seven years in the United States Army. His key leadership positions include command of the 464th Chemical Brigade and the 472nd Chemical Battalion. He has also had various military assignments including engineering and contingency contracting positions within the Korean Theater, research and development positions in the US, logistics support operations within Kuwait, and teaching chemistry at West Point. In his civilian career, Dr. Haraburda worked in various engineering positions at Bayer Corporation and G.E. Plastics, along with project management for the destruction of VX nerve agent for the US Army. He earned a BS in chemistry in 1983 from Central Michigan University, a MS in chemical engineering in 1990 and a PhD in chemical engineering in 2001 from Michigan State University, along with a Master's degree in strategic studies form the US Army War College in 2006. He is also a graduate of the US Army Command and General Staff College, the US Naval Command and Staff College, and the US Air War College. Dr. Haraburda is a registered Professional Engineer in Indiana. Additionally, he published over 30 technical or management related articles, wrote a chemical engineering handbook, conducted 20 oral histories, and gave over a dozen technical or conference presentations. He was also awarded two US patents, along with having an additional seven patent publications. He was a 2007 Examiner for the Malcolm Baldrige National Quality Award and was on the Board of Directors for the Terre Haute Children's Museum. He and his wife, the former Katherine M. Ten Have, reside in Clinton, Indiana. They have three children, Beverly, Jessica, and Christine.

www.ingramcontent.com/pod-product-compliance
Lightning Source LLC
Chambersburg PA
CBHW022134170526
45157CB00004B/1871